M000209754

THE GAME THAT ALMOST
BROKE ME

BY

TAVARSKI
"TAZ"
WALLACE

The Game That Almost Broke Me
Copyright © 2018 by Tavarski Wallace

All rights reserved. No part of this publication may be reproduced, distributed, or transmitted in any form or by any means, including photocopying, recording, or other electronic or mechanical methods, without the prior written permission of the author, except in the case of brief quotations embodied in critical reviews and certain other noncommercial uses permitted by copyright law.

For information about this title or to contact the author:
Tavarski Wallace
Email: thegtabm@gmail.com
Published: 2018
Edited by: Erin Waters
Cover Design by: Brandi Doane McCann

ISBN: 978-1-54393-204-1

Dedication

This book is dedicated

to the memory of my loving granny,

Willie D. Wallace.

1937-2017

May she rest in Heaven.

~

ACKNOWLEDGMENTS

I would like to thank my beautiful daughters Londyn and Evie for always keeping things in perspective for me. I'll always try to be an "ELITE" dad to you both. You are my motivation to do more and continue to grow. I'm very proud of you both because you are always full of life and you force me out of my comfort zone, from wearing tiaras to turning cartwheels in the living room. I will always have high expectations for you because I don't know any other way. I love you both very much. I would also like to thank my wife Rachel for being a great mother and stepmother to the girls and always being supportive regardless of my crazy ideas that sometimes don't work.

I'm very thankful for everyone that took the time to give me feedback on my story. I really appreciate you all. Your feedback really allowed me to grow and share more.

Special thanks to my mother Jacqueline Wallace for not giving up on me when I gave you every reason to give up. Thank you for always doing your best and being a great mother.

I learned a lot from you about how to treat people and the respect you instilled in me at a young age really stuck with me even during my rebellious years. I am instilling those same values in my kids.

I would like to thank all of the coaches that have spent time molding me and helping me become a better person. I really appreciate all of the sacrifices you made and I hope that I can pay it forward by giving back to the game of football and hopefully inspiring young men to be "ELITE" individuals. Special thanks to Jim Lyall and Aaron Klotz—you had a huge impact on my life at the right time and I'll be forever grateful. I want you to know that I really cherish our relationships.

Finally, I would like to thank all of my teammates. I love you all, and although we may not talk on a regular basis, please know that I'm always here for you. I miss the camaraderie we shared; there is no other sport that can bring people together like the game of football. We won a lot of games, we've struggled together in our personal lives, we attended funerals together, and we've been in each other's weddings, and it was all because of the game of football. I'm very fortunate to have so many guys that I can call brothers. Bulldogs Forever!

Thank you and I love you all!

Life is about relationships.

TABLE OF CONTENTS

CHAPTER 1

CHILDHOOD

I GREW UP IN TUSCALOOSA, Alabama, at 32C McKenzie Court, a popular housing project. Although the environment was not the greatest, I had a very loving mother and grandmother. My grandmother would do anything for me without any questions and she was very protective of all her grandkids and in her eyes we could do no wrong. My mom always put her kids first and made sure we were taken care of no matter what and we certainly had what we needed, maybe not all of the expensive things that we wanted but we definitely had what we needed. I have an older sister, Angelica, so I was the baby of the family. I was taught to love people regardless of their race, which was an important lesson to be learned in the south. It was one of the most valuable lessons I learned in my household. It wasn't about what a person had or didn't have; it was more about how they treated me and the people around me.

Our day-to-day life was pretty normal. I always thought about how I would get out of the projects and help my mom. The plan was simple: play football for the Alabama Crimson Tide and then go on to play in the NFL. I recall my mom working extremely hard as a nursing assistant. There was never a day that I worried about where my next meal was going to come from, which was not the case for some of our neighbors. Although we lived in the projects, I did not have to deal with a mother who was addicted to drugs or alcohol. Seeing people who did have to live that way still had an impact on my life. The role models in my neighborhood were drug dealers. I'm not calling them bad people, but that was the reality of our environment.

I saw my surroundings as a negative image on a daily basis. I always viewed that world as a way *not* to live, things *not* to do. My cousin Willie and I promised each other we would never be addicted to drugs, because we saw the crack addicts roaming the streets so often. I believe this was a defining time in establishing my solid foundation as an individual.

My mom, Jacqueline Wallace, always told me not to be a follower. Most thought there were only two ways out of the projects: death or jail. I was not an angel by any stretch. I remember hanging out in the service drive and being searched by the police, because a lot of the drug activity took place there. We were innocent kids in the wrong place at the wrong time.

Growing up, my neighborhood was a gold mine of negative things, and I always tried to focus on doing well in school and playing baseball, basketball, and football with the neighborhood kids. I needed to be involved with something positive. I attended Martin Luther King Jr. Elementary School, and I was very proud to be a student there, because I felt surrounded by people who understood and cared about me. However, I was not always on my best behavior. I recall going to the principal's office on several occasions, and in those days discipline was a paddling by the principal.

McKenzie Court made me tough, caring, appreciative, and thankful. I was not in the suburbs across town, but I was definitely loved, and I was very thankful for what I had. The west side of Tuscaloosa was known as the place where people who didn't have a lot of money lived. My mom had a "million dollar" work ethic, and her love was and still is priceless.

But she was also too protective at times. I had always played tackle football in the neighborhood growing up, and it was always my dream to play football for the University of Alabama. Alabama had so much tradition, with great coaches like Bear Bryant and Gene Stallings. I had my eyes on the prize and nothing was going to stop me, or so I thought. I didn't know that there would be issues playing Pop Warner football, but there were. Until this particular time, my mom had always been very supportive of the things that I wanted to do, and she always figured out a way to get me the things that I needed for sports.

CHAPTER 2

YEARNING FOR THE GAME

I WAS READY TO GRADUATE from the pick-up football games and take it to the next level. I figured it would be pretty easy, but boy, was I wrong. My mom was not excited about me wanting to play for the Westside Raiders, one of the best programs in Tuscaloosa. To be completely honest, she told me "no" every time I asked. I was relentless in my pursuit to get a "yes."

I was excited and I was going to find a way to join the team, so my solution was that I would work somehow and earn money to pay the registration fee. I presented that idea to my mom, and she told me that it didn't matter who paid, because I was not playing football.

The "WSR" won and they won often. Coach Landrum was a tough coach, and he was hard on his teams. I started to wander over to their practice field on the weekends, because it was held at Westlawn Middle School, which was a five minute walk from McKenzie Court.

Coach Landrum asked me why I wasn't playing, and I told him that my mom said that I couldn't. "Why not?" he asked. I responded that she didn't want me to get hurt, but I really wanted to play. I wanted so badly to be a part of the team, because I loved the game, and again, playing for Alabama was my dream. For the next few weeks, attending the practices at Westlawn became standard. Giving up on my chance to play was not an option.

After one practice that I attended, Coach Landrum said he would come to my home to speak with my mother, but there was some hesitation on my part. I could be in a lot of trouble having the coach come over after my mom had already told me that I couldn't play football. I told Coach Landrum that I would let him know at the next practice.

Once again, I took the five-minute walk to practice, but this time Coach Landrum was going home with me, and he would try to convince my mom to let me play football. I must admit I didn't like his chances, but I was okay with doing whatever it took to get on that field. We took the short trip to my home after practice, and I knew it was going to be either good or really bad. Coach Landrum started by telling my mom that he thought I was a good kid and how football could help me. My mom expressed her concern about me being injured because she thought that I was too small. Coach went on to say that he would take care of me on and off the field. Finally, my mom said that I could give it a try and that if I got hurt I would be done playing forever.

There was one thing I was certain about, I was not going to get hurt, and if I did, my mom would not find out unless it was a serious injury. I could not wait to get to practice. A few days later, that game that I had been yearning for was now reality, and I was not going to waste the opportunity. Some of my friends that I played basketball with on our YMCA basketball team also played football, and we were competitive.

The pads were on, and we were learning to play as a team. I played quarterback and linebacker, but my favorite position was definitely linebacker. I loved to hit people, and I hated losing, and that hasn't changed . I simply just liked the contact and it was a way for me to release aggression and because of that I became a ferocious player. I couldn't wait to get home from school so that I could go to football practice, because I was working toward my dream. The environment that surrounded me and my dreams were completely different, and I had every intention of doing the right things so that I could be successful.

The first win was a great feeling, and I knew that we had earned it because of the work we put in during the week. I developed a killer instinct because of the success we had on the field. We won, and we won a lot, receiving several first-place trophies for being the best team in our league. I was selected to play in the youth all-star game, Tuscaloosa County versus Cottondale. What a great experience! I went from begging my mom to play to playing in the all-star game.

We learned so much from our coaches about working hard and being good people. We won because they were tough on us and held us accountable regardless of how good we were or thought we were. The values of accountability, commitment, hard work, perseverance, and dedication were something that we learned at a young age, and it was understood by everyone that we were expected to live up to those values on a daily basis.

There was a lot of talent on the team, and most of us didn't have dads at home to show us right from wrong. There were not very many two-parent homes in my area. There were a lot of single mothers also playing the role of the dad and doing their best to make it. Not for one minute was I going to attempt to use that as an excuse for any behavior that was not appropriate. If we got in trouble in school, Coach Landrum knew, and we were going to hear about it at practice.

The game that I had always loved was teaching me to be disciplined and respectful. Initially I just loved hitting people. I learned really fast that the game had so much more to offer me. In fact, it had everything I needed.

CHAPTER 3

LIFE CHANGING

FAST FORWARD TO MIDDLE school. It's the start of eighth grade, and I was ecstatic because football season has started. We are practicing and things are going well, as we have a lot of guys competing for playing time. Most of us had played together since we were nine years old.

Our middle school practices reminded me of our West Side Raider days—fast and physical. We beat each other up every practice. The guys loved to see me and one of my teammates go at it, as we were two of the hardest hitters on the team, so most of the time we would circle up for the old Oklahoma drill at the end of practice.

There was a problem. I was not working as hard in the classroom as I was on the field. My mom was very disappointed that I was making poor choices. After football season, one thing led to another, and I started skipping school and making more poor choices. I was very disrespectful to my teachers as well, and that was not acceptable in my house. My mom and grandmother expected me to have respect for adults: "yes, ma'am" and "no, ma'am."

I was going down a road that could derail all of my dreams, and it was happening fast. After football season, I didn't care about many things. My coach told me that I would be dead or in jail by twenty-one if I didn't change. I was angry with him; I couldn't believe he would say those things to me. This person that I thought cared about me was telling me that I would be dead or in jail if I didn't change. It took me years to understand that he did care about me—that was exactly why he said those things.

At that time I didn't give a damn about what anyone had to say. I was going to do what I wanted and when I wanted to do it. I was making all of the choices that my mom and grandmother had raised me not to make. I was skipping school on a daily basis and not doing any work. When I did attend class, I was being kicked out of or suspended from school regularly because of the disrespect I showed toward teachers and administrators.

The impact that I was having on others wasn't clear to me, or maybe it was, but I didn't care. McKenzie Court had molded me into a good person, and I chose to go in the right direction, or so I thought. I was becoming everything that I had worked so hard to not become. My behavior and goals were not congruent, and that was a problem.

My behavior in school was starting to be disruptive to everyone involved, classes could not be taught, and I was forcing my mom to leave a job she desperately needed to pick me up, because I chose to be disrespectful and skip school. It wasn't very often that I made it through a full week of school throughout the school year. I was being suspended for three to five days at a time for my disruptive behavior.

My mom attempted to have my father step in, but I didn't fear him, because I didn't see him often, even though this was the time he was the most involved in my life. However, it was from a distance, and I didn't really give a damn about what he thought either. I was forced to talk to him and he asked if he needed to come to Tuscaloosa, although he resided in Detroit at the time. My response was "I don't care what you do." I simply didn't care about anything, and I certainly didn't see the light at the end of the tunnel. I was self-destructing, and it was happening fast.

CHAPTER 4

REALITY

THE LAST STRAW CAME when I skipped class and showed up for the school picture later in the day. I was confronted by the principal and security guard, and things immediately took a turn for the worse. When asked where I had been, I responded, "It doesn't matter where the hell I was." Being suspended was a common occurrence for me at this time, so I expected it. However, it was different this time: my mom was called to the school again, but I would also have a hearing before the Tuscaloosa City Board of Education with Mr. Croom, the Coordinator of Attendance and Student Services. He was a former football player for Alabama he was big and intimidating.

Mr. Croom had zero tolerance for kids misbehaving in school. I didn't know that everything that I was doing at Eastwood was being reported to Mr. Croom and I certainly had a reputation. Despite this, I didn't care who I was in front of or what they had to say about me. In my mind, I had life all figured out and I didn't need adults showing me the ropes. During our meeting, I was asked about my behavior, but I really didn't give any in depth responses, which didn't sit well.

It didn't take Mr. Croom long to make his decision—the verdict was in. I would be attending Tuscaloosa Alternative Learning Center, also known as TALC. It didn't really bother me because most of the guys that I hung out with attended TALC. The carefree days were over—the choice had been made for me. I could attend the alternative school as long as I wanted and if I wanted to continue to do things my way it would be for a long time.

There was a dress code: blue slacks, a white dress shirt, and black dress shoes. Once again, I put my mom in a tough predicament, forcing her to purchase new uniforms because I couldn't behave in a regular school. Monday morning was fast approaching and transportation was not provided. Therefore, I had to find my own ride to school. Luckily, one of my friends at the time had just been sent to TALC as well, so his mom was willing to give me a ride.

When I arrived at school, we had to walk through metal detectors, and I felt as if I was incarcerated. I was in one class all day and there were strict rules. Everyone started on level 1, and the ultimate goal was to get to level 4 which meant you would be transitioning and going back to a public school. My dreams of playing college football were gone at this time, and there was a strong possibility that I would be playing in my dreams behind bars—if anywhere.

On level 1, you were only allowed to have white milk with a regular lunch, and you could not purchase anything extra. The teacher was very clear that either you do what you are asked or you remain on level 1. Indeed, I hated everything about Tuscaloosa Alternative Learning Center and I would do whatever it took to get out. I was miserable every morning that I had to walk through that metal detector and go to gym class in khakis and a dress shirt, we were only allowed to change our shoes and I can tell you that attire wasn't fun in the Tuscaloosa heat. There was nobody to be mad at other than myself. My mom had done everything she could to help me go down the right path, and I rebelled. She was working hard to take care of me and I repaid her by failing to do the things she had taught me.

The lightbulb finally went off, and it was time to get out of this place that I dreaded going to so much. My goal of reaching level 4 so that I could leave the program became stronger. During the process, I even brought home a few awards for my performance in the classroom and being that my mom didn't have a lot to be proud of during those days, those awards were hung on the wall. I did the things that I needed to do to get back to regular school and would enter ninth grade at Central High School on the west campus.

After years of living in Mckenzie Court we were able to move to a house on Johnson Rd that we moved from after several years because the landlord didn't want to fix some of the problems with the house. So back to an apartment, this time we moved across the street from McKenzie court and it was a little better. I could walk to school and I was looking to start the year off the right way, and avoid going back to see Mr. Croom. My second chance was here, and it was up to me to take advantage of it.

My good friend Aaron Bonner would always tell me, "'T', you need to straighten up." He wasn't perfect, but school was a priority for him. AB was always honest and sometimes I didn't like what he had to say, but our friendship was built on truth. We loved chasing the girls together, and we never got into any trouble for doing that. I would skip school and AB's favorite thing to say was "what's up man" and "you have to chill out," with that laid-back California accent of his. Although I had people like AB trying to keep me on track, I was very stubborn and I still made poor decisions. I had to tell my boy that things were about to change.

CHAPTER 5

LEAVING HOME

Things were not going as planned. Playing football and the dream of going to the University of Alabama were fading away by the day. My friends were doing the right things and I was in limbo after going back to skipping school and not caring about my grades. To be honest, I was really selfish at the time and I only cared about me. I certainly didn't consider the negative impact that I was having on everyone else.

The summer of 1999 would change my life forever. My Uncle Lester came to visit from Michigan and at 15 years old I asked my mom if I could go live with him in Michigan. This was a very tough decision for my mom, she knew that I was heading in a direction that at some point she would be unable to help me in any way. As one could imagine, allowing your 15-year-old to leave your home would be difficult for any parent. I would probably be dead or in jail if I didn't leave my current situation because I continued to do the same things over and over again. I have never blamed my actions on my circumstances or the people around me. I made those choices and I also knew that I needed to get away. I'm so thankful my mom said yes as it was life changing.

She agreed reluctantly to allow me to move to Adrian, Michigan. I packed my bags and I was ready for the new journey and it was a much needed journey. I had three days before we would leave and I was hoping that my mom wouldn't change her mind within those three days. I know my mom struggled with letting me go. She wrote me a letter and explained that it was very hard to be away from me. Unfortunately, there were people in my family that felt she made the wrong decision, and I believe she knew if she didn't let me go she wouldn't have a son, which scared her as it would any parent. I'm very thankful that she did what was best for me even though it didn't feel right at the time. The things that I regret are the things that allowed me to grow and become a better person.

It was tough for me as well. Tuscaloosa was the only thing I knew and I loved living in the south, so I struggled with the move. I was a 15-year-old that was still wet behind the ears and I had to grow up fast. I'm a blue collar guy because of the place that I still call home today. I desperately wanted to be successful there and I just didn't get it done.

CHAPTER 6

ONLY OPTION

I HAD BEEN KICKED OUT of school and sent to an alternative school. I was still making poor choices in Tuscaloosa and something bad was going to happen. I became aware of the life that I was starting to live, and something needed to change. The same kid that loved football had forgotten about his childhood dreams and started to be a part of his negative environment instead of being the one that would make it out and become an example to others.

I often thought about the people that had invested so much time in to me with the hopes that I would be successful, including the coaches with the West Side Raiders and my coaches at the YMCA for basketball and baseball. They had done so much to try and teach us to be young men through sports and I was disappointing them all including my mom and grandmother.

Being the person I was becoming was never part of the plan. I was determined to change my current situation. Through the trials and tribulation, I didn't really care about where I played anymore. I needed to finish high school, go to college and play football. This was my only way out, and I was running out of opportunities.

It was time to look myself in the mirror. I've always known right from wrong, and it was time to use better judgement. I had seen so many guys from Tuscaloosa have so much potential and do nothing with it because of the choices that they made.

CHAPTER 7

ROAD TRIP

The 12-hour trip to Michigan was a long journey. Finally we arrived to my uncle's home and the environment was completely different. In Tuscaloosa, I had always felt it was about surviving. Everything was different from the community to the schools, and I had to make new friends.

The reality was that it was a new place, but there were still plenty of opportunities to get in trouble if that's what I wanted to do. The first thing was to decide which school I was going to attend and the first choice was Madison High School. It was a lot smaller than my last school. We needed to go and enroll so that I could start working out with the football team.

While enrolling, I was told that since I didn't have enough credits. I needed to take a summer school course if I wanted to be in 9th grade—and I definitely wanted to be in high school. I would be taking the summer school class with Coach Hamilton. He was a serious guy and he didn't play around. Right away I knew that he cared about me. I would pick up my assignments after weight lifting and he would give me a deadline. Coach Hamilton is someone that

I still have a relationship with to this day. He went out of his way on multiple occasions to help me out and make sure I was doing the right things.

From a football prospective, I could tell most of the guys' approach was a little different than what I was used to. We would have about 10-15 guys who would show up on a consistent basis, and that was not okay. In Tuscaloosa, if you played football you worked out and there was no discussion. There may not have been a lot of guys, but there were definitely good guys.

The weight room is where I met Jeremy and Robbie Roesch—two brothers who believed in working hard. They had a wonderful mom who was always very welcoming. Not only did they work hard, but they were good students and they had goals. It didn't take us long to become close friends. I had one thing in common with them and that was the love for the game of football. Robbie and Jeremy really helped me develop that same love for school. We hung out a lot and it was apparent that they were people that I needed to be around. The summer went on and the Roesch brothers would pick me up for lifting and whatever else we had in the summer. They really helped me with the transition to a new school. I'm not sure what I would've done without them.

We were getting close to the end of the summer and I had a few more assignments to turn in to Coach Hamilton before I was officially in 9th grade and eligible to play football. The new school year started and I was beyond excited. I was back doing what I loved, and this time I had a greater appreciation for school and understood that I couldn't just play football but I had to be a student-athlete.

The first week went well and as the second week started I was confident that my run-ins with teachers were over, but that wasn't the case. I was back in the principal's office, this time at a new school where I was supposed to have a fresh start. Once again I was being disrespectful to a teacher by refusing to do my work. After several attempts to get me to complete the assignment, I told the teacher I wasn't doing anything and to stop talking to me. What do you know? I was suspended again, and this time it was for the remainder of the day. Here I was with a great opportunity, and I was already sabotaging it within weeks.

That was it and it would be the last time that I was suspended from school. I could not continue to let my family down in Tuscaloosa and my new family in Michigan. I had finally arrived as a person and things were going great. I had adapted to my new school. Everything that I had gone through had prepared me to be successful. I completed the school year without another incident and I was going to tenth grade.

CHAPTER 8

━━━

HOME SICK

There was a problem. I was homesick. I wanted to go back to Tuscaloosa. Although I knew this wasn't the best decision, I still wanted to return home. The staff at Madison tried very hard to convince me not to go back, but my mind was set and I was going home. My basketball coach Mr. Anschuetz called me in his office to talk some sense into me but it didn't work. I booked a greyhound bus ticket and I was going home to the place where I had made so many poor choices over and over again. I went back to Central High School and I would start working out with the football team again. I was ready to get my license and that meant getting a car. In Alabama when you turned sixteen you went to the Secretary of State to take the test for your license. There weren't any requirements for drivers training. I couldn't wait to go to school and do the things that were asked of me. My days of disrespecting teachers were over and I was starting to mature. I always looked forward to going over to the field house for 4th period, as all football players were required to lift.

Once again I was getting in the swing of things and this time actually doing well in school. I got my first job at Church's Chicken, thanks to my sister Angelica. I've always liked to work and make my own money and that started at a young age. I loved making money, and I even used to sell candy bags in the neighborhood because of it. Things were looking up— I was working and soon I would be taking the driver's test for my license and hopefully getting a car. Even during times of my disruptive behavior, I've always been a hard worker. My mom told me that she would help me get a car with some of her tax return and the money that I was making at Church's. Finally I got my first car for $800. It was a tan Buick and I gave it the name "deuce and a quarter." My wonderful granny bought me a set of 8x10 speakers and detachable CD player for my new ride. I was happy to be driving to school and having the freedom to go when I wanted to.

Too much freedom lead to me getting involved in things that could land me in the juvenile detention center. I was put on probation and the license that I had just received was gone. Once again, I found a way to ruin the things that I had going for myself. I literally had to be in the house when the street lights came on as it was part of my probation. I continued to be on probation for six months and it was a long six months. It was awful and I just knew that they only told me six months to scare the hell out me. I hated checking in with my probation officer and calling to verify that I was in the house on time. They made it very clear to me that it was zero tolerance and if I wanted spend time locked up, go out and violate probation. For once in my young life I decided to follow my probation as expected because being locked up just didn't sound fun to me.

After getting off of probation and going back to Michigan and leaving again, (that's right, I left Michigan twice) I was finally back in Adrian. This time when I returned to Adrian I decided to move in with a few of my teammates from high school Aaron and Justin for a year, their mom Barb welcomed me with open arms. Aaron and I shared a room and we were definitely like brothers. Barb treated me as if I was her son and I was thankful to have a mother figure in Michigan. I never returned to live in Tuscaloosa. I finished my high school football career and graduated from Madison High and received the Principal's Award. It was time to make a decision about college football.

The transferring back and forth did have an effect on my high school career and I was not able to play as a senior. So, I really had two options: East Central Community College or Adrian College. I had already taken my ACT test and I applied to both places. I needed to make a decision and a great man by the name of Jim Lyall helped me make that decision.

Coach Lyall called me often during my senior of high school, even though I didn't play one down during that year. The care that he showed for me made me want to attend Adrian College, and that was what I did. Coach Lyall showed that he cared about me as a person and he wanted to help me be successful and get a degree. I had come a long way in the last few years but I definitely still had work to do.

CHAPTER 9

TRAGEDY

In 2003 DURING MY freshman year in college, I received awful news. One of my friends from Tuscaloosa had been murdered at a night club. I couldn't wrap my head around this. Phillip was a good person and he had lost his life at the age of 18. Phil was a very likable person and he had a big heart. He was attending Shelton State University and I always knew he would be a successful person. He was attending school for welding. Unfortunately he was never able to fulfill his dreams. Fast-forward three years to 2006 and I received awful news again. Another friend had been murdered at the age of 21. Immediately I broke down in tears. How could this be happening? James was my guy—we went to school together and hung out a lot when he was allowed to come out. We always gave "JB" as we called him a hard time, because his dad was pretty strict.

We lived really close to each other; JB would come to my house on Johnson Rd. before school to pick me up on his Ninja motorcycle so that we could ride the same bus to school. I remembered all of the good times we had and the trouble we sometimes got into.

There is not a day that goes by that I don't think about Phil & JB. They were the last people that I thought would be taken at such a young age. I would use these two negative and hurtful situations to change my life. I had been so negative and did a lot of things that could have put me in a bad situation, and these two respectful guys were gone. I truly miss those guys and I wish their families never had to lose them.

I couldn't control what happened to Phil and JB, but I could try to make myself a better person. I was still trying to establish my identity and I would certainly be lying if I said their deaths didn't bother me. I've always been somewhat of a guarded and reserved person and still to this day there are certain places I don't like to be because of their deaths. I don't like very large crowds, bars, or clubs. Death is something that is a part of life, but losing them changed me to a certain extent.

CHAPTER 10

NEW CHALLENGE

Dᴜʀɪɴɢ ᴛʜᴇ ʀᴇᴄʀᴜɪᴛɪɴɢ ᴘʀᴏᴄᴇss, Coach Lyall told me that he could promise me two things: that I would get a great education and compete for championships. When I arrived at Adrian College, my dream of playing college football was now a reality. Although I had dreams of playing at the college level, now it was about more than just football for me. I wanted to become a better man and son. I didn't have a father figure until I arrived on campus at Adrian College. There, I was fortunate enough to have two father figures—Jim Lyall and Aaron Klotz, our Defensive Coordinator.

My entire time in college I watched how these two men in particular treated people, including their wives and kids. Even though I didn't know everything or expected them to be perfect, I observed them any and every chance that I saw them around their wife and kids. I had the opportunity to watch them be husbands and fathers. I also had the opportunity to experience Coach Klotz becoming a dad for the first time, and I still cherish those relationships to this day. They did not always tell me what I wanted to hear, but they did always tell me what I needed to hear. I was taking advantage of my opportunities now instead of sabotaging them. There wasn't a chance in hell that I was going to blow this opportunity, as I was living the dream and playing college football.

Things did not go my way when I was a freshman at Adrian College in 2003. During one of our practices, I got into an argument with one of the GA's. I was walking off the field because I was done playing and putting up with him when Coach Lyall intervened and I returned to practice. I believe there were some choice words from Coach Lyall to the GA and I was happy to not be on the receiving end. During my freshman year I thought that I should be moved up to varsity because we also had a JV team and the coaches thought another linebacker was the guy to move up and I didn't agree with it but I respected and trusted those guys. I quickly learned that it wasn't about me and in that instance I really began to embrace the "it's all about the team" approach. They taught me more about life than football. I understood that things were not always going to go my way and I had to learn to deal with adversity or I wouldn't make it in college football or life for that matter. Failure is only failure when you do nothing to change the current circumstances.

Going into the summer before my sophomore season, I didn't complain about the other linebacker being moved up instead of me. I made my mind up that I was going to out-work him and I would be playing on Saturdays. I emailed Coach Klotz and I told him that I wanted to be the greatest leader, greatest middle linebacker that had ever played at Adrian and the school's all-time leading tackler. I'm sure he thought I was crazy. After all, this email was coming from a guy that had never started one down on Saturdays and spent most of his time playing JV as a freshman. I had that much confidence in my ability that I was willing to send that email. I trained all summer with

Joel Howland, who had seen some time on varsity as a freshman. Joel attended Adrian High School and we met at Adrian College and became workout partners and eventually we were like brothers. One summer I moved in to his mother's house so that we could keep our same workout schedule. We truly cared for each other. He was my guy and still is to this day. We competed and pushed each other to the limit in everything thing that we did. We didn't have a buddy system when it was time to work— we understood our purpose and we were working to be the best. Summer was winding down and it was almost show time.

My sophomore year is when I started to make a name for myself, I held myself and teammates to a very high standard and we were going to operate a certain way as a unit and it didn't matter to me if you were a junior or senior. The guys I played with knew I cared about them and I felt the same about them and when there is trust you can push guys and make them uncomfortable.

CHAPTER 11

CAMP

THE DAY HAD COME and I showed up pissed off— not at anyone in particular, but I was on a mission to be exactly what I had referenced in my email to Coach Klotz at the beginning of the summer. We showed up to check-in for camp and the linebacker that played varsity as a freshman didn't come back to school. I was still on a mission and I was going to destroy anything in my path. I wasn't hoping to be the best, I would be the best. That confidence came from one intangible quality that always separates the best–great work ethic. Everything I did in the off-season was to start the journey off becoming great. I was not interested in being friends with anyone on the practice field. I absolutely loved practice because I wanted to perfect my craft. I also cared about being a good teammate off the field and there were plenty of guys who were not sure if I liked them because of the way I approached practice. The football field was my sanctuary: no matter what was going on in my life, when I stepped on the grass I was able to lock in and work at a high level each and every day. This required a certain mental approach and a desire to be great. I had been through a lot to even to have a chance to be playing at the college level. I had come a long way from the kid who had to beg his mom to play. My career took off as a sophomore, and before every game I would write "mom" on my wrist tape to remind myself why I was doing what I was doing. I recorded 155 tackles in 10 games and received an award from the NCAA for the most solo tackles (100) in a season. As one can imagine, there is a price to pay for playing such a physical game. However, I loved every minute of it and I was definitely willing to pay the price.

After my sophomore season I needed surgery because of a torn labrum and bicep tendon. I injured my shoulder halfway through the season during a game in which I recorded over 30 tackles. Coach Lyall put a red jersey on me the following week for one practice after the injury to slow me down, but it didn't help. I only had one speed and I am a firm believer that you play how you practice. He told me after practice, I can't protect you if you're going to go full contact with a red jersey on so we got rid of the red jersey because I didn't want to wear it. It was a painful injury, but I refused to miss a practice or game, since we were having a great season and every game counted. My fingers would tingle and my left arm would go numb after the first hit in every practice and game. I wasn't looking to miss practice and I knew it was something I just had to deal with. I wanted to win and I knew my teammates needed me, so there was no way that I was going to have surgery during the season.

After the season I had surgery, and the fun started. My teammates would come over in the mornings to help me get dressed, and after the first day of helping me they were complaining that they were doing a lot of work to get me ready for the day I would rehab with our trainer and he pushed me as he always did. I would also go in to do legs in the weight room because I obviously couldn't do upper body.

My shoulder surgery was no excuse for missing the weight room. It was a long 4-6 month process to rehab. After I was cleared, I worked even harder. The last thing I wanted to be was a one hit wonder. I had learned that consistency was the key to being successful regardless of what you were doing. I now had a responsibility and people could count on me without any hesitation. I embraced that role for the first time in my life. I loved my teammates and I expected them to work hard. Although I had a dream, my number one priority was to be a great teammate because I knew that what we had at Adrian College was special. I also knew that I would be scratching and clawing when I left college to get on a roster, and I was okay with that. This wasn't anything new to me because I had scratched and clawed my entire life.

During my junior year, I was voted as one of the captains, which was a great honor. Being a captain was something I took a great deal of pride in. Before the season we decided as a group that we wouldn't go out on Thursday nights which was a popular night to be out. During the season, one of our senior outside linebackers decided to disregard that rule and myself and the other captains decided to bench him for half of the next game. Every guy in the locker room including myself was held to a high standard, and it didn't matter if you were an All-American or a 4th string running back. I cherished my teammates and I was willing to do whatever it took to win, even if that meant getting after a senior for not doing things the right way. The kid from Tuscaloosa that had made so many mistakes was being asked to lead a group of young men. I had learned so much from everything that had taken place in my life prior to attending college. I would often tell my teammates to never take things for granted, as I had grown up around people that would die to be in our position.

When I walked around campus, some people's perception of me was that I was mean or I was arrogant. This couldn't have been any farther from the truth. However, I was very arrogant on the field and I wasn't ashamed of that. I didn't say a lot as I was truly taking in everything that was happening around me. The guy that went from playing JV was now an All-American. Becoming an All-American would've never happened without my coaches and teammates. I was so thankful that Coach Lyall was in my corner. I really valued the relationships that I built on campus and maybe I didn't come across as someone that was approachable, but I certainly enjoyed the people around me.

I would always stop in to see Coach Lyall and Coach Klotz, the energetic one. They were the ones that cared about me when other coaches didn't. They believed in me during a time when I didn't really believe in myself. They saw something in me years before I saw it and I was very thankful that they had stayed by my side. The coaches sacrificed so much to provide us with the best opportunities possible. There wasn't a scholarship but there was a lot of damn love and a few father figures that I needed in the worst way. The game of football saved me from being a statistic, and quite honestly it was where I felt the best as a person. I gave the game every ounce of me and I mean everything I had was given to the game of football.

CHAPTER 12

D3

DIVISION 3 ATHLETICS: THE land and arena where most go to get an education and close out their athletic careers. I was a little different, though. I didn't want any part of closing out my career at Adrian College—it was my dream to play in the NFL and I was not going to change it just because my dream of playing at the University of Alabama didn't come true. Just like I didn't give up after all of the hurdles I had put in my own way. It's not about where you're coming from but about where you're going. I had a burning desire to be successful, and no matter how many mistakes I made, I never lost sight of where I wanted to go. I certainly didn't have any time for hoping; instead, I put all of my energy into working.

My Uncle Earl told me that he would support me through college as long as I was playing football. Uncle Earl had grown up in the same environment and he went on to college and later became a police officer and detective. He understood what it took to be successful and he didn't use McKenzie Court as an excuse to be unsuccessful. With his and my mom's support, I was able to focus on school and football.

I was fortunate enough to play with guys that had been through a lot of adversity throughout their lives. We thrived off of each other and made each other better. When the Bulldogs came to town, everyone knew that we would be physical and a little arrogant on the field, which was just how we operated as a unit. We were proud of the way that we played. My fellow linebacker AJ and I received the nickname Salt and Pepper for obvious reasons, we were two guys that competed all the time and we made each other better.

Division 3 football taught me so much about life. There were no scholarships, so most players on our team had a love for the game that was unmatchable, which was the beauty of playing at our level. We cared about each other and we had a lot great coaches that loved their players. There is not enough credit given to the D3 student athletes, because we are not on TV. We worked extremely hard to be successful within our program.

I stopped going back home to Tuscaloosa in the summer so that I could stay in Adrian and work out. I would go out and run and do agilities on my own because I wanted to be great. I had one goal on Saturdays, and that was to punish anyone that touched the ball. Mentally, I would go to the darkest place possible before the game.

On Fridays I wouldn't see anyone after practice and dinner, I would put my Ray Lewis "Beyond the Glory" VHS in and zone out. I would make things up in my mind about the opponents and I was beyond angry and pissed off on game day. I was arrogant and I didn't have any problem talking trash on the field.

I was not an arrogant guy off of the field, but when it was game day my personality changed completely. I would talk to running backs before the game and tell them exactly what I was going to do to them for four quarters. I appreciated every snap that I took; I had taken so much for granted and almost blew any opportunity to be where I was.

We all have choices in life and sometimes we make the right ones and sometimes we don't. I made a lot of bad choices, but I did not start to flourish until I made those bad choices and could grow from them.

During my career, my dad had choices as well and it's something that he has to live with. I had played a ton of high school football games and the guy that was my biological father never saw me play one down in high school. I made 429 tackles in college and he saw 10 in one half of a game that we blew our opponent out. I finished my career as the NCAA Division 3 All-Time leading tackler per game. He lived an hour away and saw me play once. It bothered me that what I was doing wasn't important to him, so in return that anger was taken out on my opponents every Saturday. I wanted to inflict pain on the opposition, and that's how I played the game. It was never "poor me". I love my dad because he was a part of bringing me into this world. We don't have a relationship today and that's okay. I am my own man, and you won't find me missing anything that my kids are involved in.

I was the school's all-time leading tackler after shattering the previous record of 289 tackles, and an All-American. I always thought about my email that I sent to Coach Klotz and man did I live that email. I accomplished everything that I referenced in that email. I don't know if I'm the greatest linebacker to ever play at Adrian College, but for four years I told myself that I was. I had come from the bottom to the top and every day that I stepped on the field it was all business. Coach Deere was my position coach and he would always ask me why I was so serious before practice. I would always replay the struggle to get where I was before practice and games and that took me to a different level mentally.

CHAPTER 13

ONE STEP CLOSER

Afterʀ ᴍʏ ᴊᴜɴɪᴏʀ sᴇᴀsᴏɴ, it was time to go under the knife again. This time it was my meniscus. I was back with our trainer and we were doing double days. We didn't have a pool at the college so we went to a local apartment complex to ask for permission to rehab in their pool. The surgery took place six weeks before the season was going to start, and again, I was not missing practice. I had recorded almost 300 tackles in two seasons. The awards and attention were pouring in, but I refused to change who I was and I didn't have time to be complacent. At the college level, if you don't want to do your job at a high level, there is always a guy behind you that will. I was still the same guy that was going to bust his ass and I cared more about my teammates than individual success. This is why I never hung up one award I received during college. I felt that if we didn't win a championship I didn't deserve to hang up any awards that I had received, and that was a promise I made to some of my teammates.

However, I was one step closer to my dream, I was called in to Coach Lyall's office and he told me that that the Detroit Lions and New York Jets wanted to come in for a junior day with me. That kid from Mckenzie Court would be meeting with NFL scouts. I was scheduled to run the 40 yard dash and take the Wonderlic Test. They were also going to meet with Coach Lyall to find out more about me and my character. During this time I had conversations with people that I could tell didn't think I had a chance in hell to play at the next level or receive any interest for that matter. They never told me directly but I could see it in their eyes and body language.

I'm not sure how many times NFL scouts had come to Adrian College to see a player. We didn't have someone on staff that specialized in the 40 yard dash. I didn't waste any time contacting a local trainer by the name of John Dillard. John was known for his work, and it was my goal to work with him to strengthen my core.

John and I came up with a game plan. It was perfect timing, as John had been recently hired as the Equipment Director at Adrian College. We would come in around 6 am and start working, and let me tell you, we worked. The last thing I wanted to do was not attack the task at hand. I was willing to do whatever it took to be prepared for the junior day, because this was what I wanted. The NFL would give me an opportunity to help my mom and that drove me.

The weeks went by and I continued my sessions with John, while doing our normal off-season workout. I was not focused on the Lions and Jets; I was focused on the work that needed to be done to receive an opportunity. It wasn't time to be caught up in the hype. I never thought that I was better than my teammates or anyone else because of the opportunities that I had. I had worked extremely hard to be in this position and it all happened while still being humble and a good teammate. I didn't believe that I had to sacrifice how I treated people for my dreams to come true.

The night before I zoned out (as I often did before games), I watched my Ray Lewis "Beyond the Glory' VHS. It was here and I had put in a countless amount of hours for this day. I woke up early and had breakfast and prepared myself mentally for what I was about to encounter. I took the short trip over to the Merillat Sports and Fitness center where I would be running inside and taking the Wonderlic Test. A few of my closest friends and my girlfriend at the time were present. I walked in and said hello to anyone that I saw, which is something that I did on a daily basis. I would walk into the trainer's room with my headphones on to be stretched, I tell the trainers good morning and thanks for stretching me. Pastor Troy is blaring in my ears and I was on a different planet.

CHAPTER 14

———

SHOWTIME

THE SCOUTS HAD ARRIVED. I met with them in Coach Lyall's office, I looked them in their eyes and gave them a firm handshake. They asked me a few questions about the season and my health. It was time to get to business. The guys from the NFL don't waste a lot of time and I liked that it was a job interview, and that's how I approached it. The Wonderlic was a timed test. They gave me instruction after instruction and would repeat two minutes when the time was almost up for each portion of the test. If I didn't finish I had to stop wherever I was. When the test was over, it felt like I had been in the room forever.

It was time to run the 40 yard dash. We walked out of the offices and headed down the steps. I had only told a few people and there were definitely more than a few there to watch. One of the scouts said "Let's take care of business before this turns into a circus," and I agreed. I appreciated the support but I had to focus on the task at hand and not worry about who was there. I stripped down to nothing but spandex shorts and I was ready to run. I stepped to the line and I was zoned out. I got down in my stance and *boom*—I took the first step and it felt good. One down, and one to go. I approached the line again and got through the same routine. I felt more explosive on the second one. That was it—I was one step closer.

I walked over to thank my friends for their support. The scouts and I walked out together. They wished me luck during my senior year and told me to keep up the good work. I thanked them for coming and that I looked forward to hearing back from them. There wasn't a lot of small talk and I was okay with that because I was not looking for people to blow smoke. I prepared and did the things that I needed to for that particular day.

Shortly after the scouts left the school I received a call that I was going to be invited to the Magnolia Classic which was an All-Star game in Mississippi. I accepted the invitation. There were only two D3 players invited, and I was one of them. It was predominately a D1 and 1AA All-Star game. I was not going to kiss anyone's ass when I got to the game, which would take place after my senior season in college. It didn't matter to me what school guys were from – I was there to compete, and it was as simple as that.

My performance obviously provided me with another opportunity to be seen, as there would be scouts at our practices and at the game. I also understood that this was a cutthroat business, so I wasn't getting too high or too low. In my opinion, there is no loyalty in the business of football after you leave college.

Even though I was one step closer, it was time to refocus and get prepared for my senior season. I went back to work the same afternoon after the scouts left. That was just how I operated. There is no substitute for hard work and I was still on a mission. I was told a few days later that the Chicago Bears had called and requested film and they had also sent one of our assistant coaches a few apparel items. I thanked the coach for telling me. I had gone back to work fast—none of those things would be relevant if I went out and changed who I was and stopped working hard. The reality was in my mind I had accomplished nothing and playing in the NFL was still a dream that I was chasing.

I always thought that great players were great because they were consistent and were always looking for ways to get better. I wanted to be great, and "average" was not in my vocabulary. It's easy to become complacent when you are starting to be recognized. I worked so hard because I feared going back to the linebacker who didn't play.

I was receiving letters and phone calls from agents. It was all starting to be very real. I obviously couldn't sign with an agent until after my senior year. I wouldn't mention anything to people because I've never been a person that likes to bring attention to myself. If I thought someone needed to know something, I would tell them, but otherwise I wouldn't mention it. Again, my goals were to focus on my senior season and be loyal and committed to my brothers.

CHAPTER 15

LAST SEASON

Going into my last year, the expectations were high as usual—we wanted to win an MIAA championship. We opened the season with Defiance College. I had a few words with one of their receivers during the summer, after he came to our campus to check out our new stadium. I thought it took a lot of guts to show up on our campus. I confronted him and told him to leave. I didn't like any of my opponents, and he was no exception.

Unfortunately, we lost our home opener 10-7. I couldn't believe we had lost to Defiance. That was the story of our season as we finished 5-5, I was beyond disappointed we had worked so hard in the off-season to finish our college careers with a championship. I still think about things that we could have done better as a unit to avoid a 5-5 season. We expected to win every time we stepped on the field. There was no championship and the season was over that fast. I recorded over 100 tackles three years in a row.

I was upset about the outcome and not winning a championship. I didn't have much down time after the season, as it was time to decide which agent I would sign with and when I would start training. Coach Lyall arranged for me to attend the Michigan pro day. All 32 NFL teams would be there, so it was important that I was prepared. It was time to interview agents. I reached out to BJ Dean. He was from Tuscaloosa and attended Florida State, and was in camp with the Baltimore Ravens. I asked him to give me as much advice as possible about the process and he was very helpful. I had narrowed my list down to three and one of my biggest questions was how they could help me get to the next level. If they were not going to provide training, they were eliminated. I also wanted someone who was going to focus on me and the things that I needed to do to be successful.

There was an agent out of New York and he actually ran the company with his brother and they were not able to provide training so I was down to two. There was another based out of San Francisco and the other one was out of Atlanta. I had communicated with both them for quite some time. I even spoke with an offensive lineman that was playing with the Arizona Cardinals because he was represented by the company out of San Francisco, so I wanted to find out how they treated him. The agent from San Francisco flew to Michigan to meet with me after I decided to sign with him. We talked about the process for the next few months and we discussed where I would train. The original plan was for me to go to Utah to train at Velocity Sports Performance. It was clear that I was going to have to leave school so that I could focus on my preparation for the pro day.

The agent was responsible for my housing, weekly groceries, supplements, training, training clothing and it was my job to work hard. I had to make sure that I would not have to pay him back if I didn't get signed by an NFL team, he would receive 3% if I signed an

NFL contract and that was pretty standard. I had a pretty nice set-up, which most people wouldn't do for a D3 guy.

CHAPTER 16

ALL-STAR

I HAD ACCEPTED MY INVITATIONS to the two all-star games. The East Coast bowl was the first game, and it consisted of D1AA, D2, D3 and NAIA players. The East Coast Bowl featured 70 of the best Division I-AA, II, III and NAIA players from 33 different states. My coach was from the CFL. The second game was the Magnolia Gridiron Classic and it was held in Mississippi. I had the privilege of being coached by former Mississippi state head coach Jackie Sherrill. The Magnolia Classic had a plethora of D1 players from schools like Northwestern, Toledo, Syracuse, Memphis, Mississippi State, and Illinois just to name a few.

The moment my last game was over at Adrian College I didn't have much time off, as the East Coast bowl was scheduled for November 25, 2006 and the Magnolia Gridiron Classic was scheduled for December 23, 2006. The all-star games had scouts at practice and the games, and quite honestly I felt like a piece of meat. During one of the games we had to get down to our spandex and walk through by the scouts and they critiqued your build. It was an intense process, and the scouts wanted to know everything about you. There were also scouts present who didn't have any people skills at all. I recall one scout becoming upset because guys were choosing not to run the 40 yard dash after being advised by their agents. He sat us all in the bleachers and basically said that guys were not taking advantage of opportunities because they were choosing not to run. In reality we were not prepared to run as most guys had just finished their college season and didn't have any time to start training for the 40 yard dash. Anyone with knowledge about the preparation to run a fast time understands that the start and the first 10 yards will make or break your time. I certainly didn't agree with his message because no matter what, if you ran a slow time, immediately some scouts would cross you off of their list. The NFL is a "what can you do for me now" business. I chose not to run the 40 yard dash, because I was not going to be influenced by this particular scout.

After attending the games, I really began to understand some of the things that got guys in trouble. At one of our hotels, the lobby was filled with an unbelievable amount of women who were there only because the players were in town for the All-Star game. It was like a TV show: NFL teams were conducting interviews in different conference rooms at the hotel and agents were all over the place.

I was fortunate to play in both games and come out healthy. I was the leading tackler for the East Coast bowl. I had an opportunity to see family and friends at both stops. My friend TJ and his dad came to East Coast Bowl, my family and the Roesch brothers came to the game in Mississippi.

I was able to perform at a high level and I felt like I was putting myself in the right position to get an opportunity with a team and to also show the guys from the CFL that I could play on a bigger field.

CHAPTER 17

HARD WORK

We DECIDED TO STAY in Michigan for training which was a decision I later regretted. I would pack up after the All-Star games were over and head to Novi, Michigan, where I would be living in an Extended Stay for the next two months. It was time to grind.

In my opinion, the first trainer wasn't getting it done. I trained with a former Michigan player, and while it may have been working for him, it was not working for me. I didn't like the environment—my agent had paid for me to work out with the head trainer, and most of the time he wasn't there. The things that we were doing didn't make a lot of sense: we were running too many full 40 yard dashes and not focusing on the starts, which are the foundation of a good 40 time. I was training two or three times a day. I would eat, train, and do it all over again the next day.   I contacted my agent and explained to him what was going on. We didn't have time to waste money or training days. We waited a month before changing trainers, and I regret we did, because nothing changed. I was frustrated, but again I was not giving up or losing focus on the task at hand. We decided to go to Velocity Sports Performance in Canton, Michigan and it was a great environment. I trained with guys from Michigan State and the quarterback from Alma College. We were familiar with each other because Alma was in our league and we played every year. Velocity had an immediate impact on my preparation and I regretted not going there in the first place. But, you live and learn. I would grind for hours and I mean *grind*. I loved every second of it.

We ran, stretched, lifted, and did things that were awkward but we were all there with hopes of getting a shot to play in the NFL and no one needed extra motivation. I had to make sure I was taking care of my body, because it couldn't fail me. I had to eat a certain way, make sure I was getting the proper sleep, and be prepared for the things that I was going to endure each day. I had everything down to the minute when it came down to eating and taking supplements

My 40 yard dash time changed drastically and it was because the guys and their attention to detail at Velocity were second to none. I was chasing my dream and remaining humble as well. We were getting closer to our pro days and you could see it in our eyes: we were dripping with sweat and being pushed to the limit. When we finished, I would have to sit down for 5-10 minutes before going to my car because I was completely exhausted. I was giving the game everything that I had. I never wanted to cheat the game.

There were three things that we prepared for: the 40 yard dash, short shuttle, and the L drill. Those were the drills the scouts cared about. Mentally I went into the sessions as if it was a game. Entering our final sessions, it was all about fine tuning the things we had worked on. It was almost showtime. The trainer at Velocity gave me a routine to do every day leading up to the pro day and I followed his plan.

CHAPTER 18

PRO DAY

Coach Klotz drove me to the University of Michigan, as I was eating several tuna sandwiches and chugging my gallon of water to make sure I weighed in at a decent weight. All of the guys that you saw on TV were there: LaMarr Woodley, Alan Branch, Mike Hart and the rest. But I was not there to get autographs. The two guys who were so influential in my life were a huge part of getting me to the pro day. That was how they operated and I can't say enough about the love I still have for them to this day. It wasn't just about a pro day— they were also a big part of my growth.

We arrived at the University of Michigan and it was everything I expected. The facility was packed with NFL head coaches and scouts. The opportunity was everything that I had dreamed about and more. We were required to go into the locker room so that we could get instructions on how the day was going to go. When were done, I went through the same dynamic warm-up that I had gone through so many times during my workout sessions at Velocity, and 15 minutes later I was dripping sweat as usual.

This was everything I wanted. Once again, I was in front of scouts, but this time it was also Rod Marinelli, Mike Tomlin, and many more. The environment was intense. I've always thought it was interesting when you get a lot of football players in one room, the egos were bigger than the building itself, and I loved it.

The moment had come and it was time to start the testing: 40 yard dash, short shuttle, L-Drill, and position drills. It was time to sink or swim. We were being critiqued on everything including our work ethic and effort, and the coaches also wanted to see how players responded when things didn't go their way.

I can tell you that there are a lot of politics involved in the process. I'll refrain from mentioning his name but there was a Michigan linebacker that repeatedly messed up on the short-shuttle, and from what I saw it didn't appear that he wanted to be there. I got the impression that most of the guys knew they were going to get a shot whether they were drafted high or low, or brought in as an UDFA (undrafted free agent.)

I didn't have that luxury. I needed to catch someone's eye, and the preparation that went into getting ready for the pro day was taxing mentally and physically after preparing for two months straight six days a week. I went through all of my drills and I felt great. The day had come to an end and the results from the day would be posted. At this point I was getting a lot of calls from the media and those looking to do a story on the D3 kid looking to get a shot to play in the NFL.

Coach Klotz and I headed back to Adrian. The work had been done, and now it was a waiting game for the next month or so. I would speak with my agent on a regular basis, I had recorded a 4.65 40 as my best time. I wanted to run a little faster than that, but during training I had posted times of 4.6 to 4.65, so I wasn't surprised. If I didn't switch trainers I would've never posted a 4.65 as my best time and there is no doubt about it. We continued to sit and wait. My agent was making phone calls to see where I would end up because we knew that I would get a shot.

CHAPTER 19

DRAFT DAY

I TUNED IN TO THE draft as I had always done even before there was a possibility that my phone could ring. This time was a little more special and I was joined by my Uncle Lester and Joel on day two because anything could happen and if we were going to hear something, it would be on day two of the draft.

The second day was here we watched the third round, fourth round, fifth round, sixth round, and finally the 7th round was about to start. I started getting extremely nervous as I didn't want anyone to call me that was not an NFL team.

The seventh round was almost over and still nothing, I would be lying if I told you that I wasn't a little worried that my phone was not ringing as the draft was close to being over. The final pick of the draft is known as "mister irrelevant", which was announced and the draft was over. My uncle and Joel didn't really know what to say so they didn't say anything. Joel said that he was going to take off and I thanked him for sticking around and going through this stressful time with me. The draft was over and I was in disbelief that my phone didn't ring; I had sacrificed everything and committed myself to training and doing everything that I could to get a shot.

I went to sit outside at my uncle's house where I was staying at the time to get some fresh air with my phone still attached to my hand. *Ring Ring Ring!* It was a 313 number, and I answered. It was a scout from the Detroit Lions—the team that had come to see me at my Junior Day. The scout asked me how I was doing. I said that I was doing okay and I was excited to hear from him. He went on to say that they wanted to bring me in for Rookie camp and I told him that I would be there. I was beyond excited and full of emotion. I called my mom to tell her that I was invited to the Detroit Lions Rookie Camp. After speaking to my mom my agent had called and I told him the Lions had just called. Although there was excitement, we knew they were loaded with linebackers, and if all failed we would have film to show other NFL teams.

I gave Joel a call and headed over to see my guys at AC. I pulled up to the College View apartments and a lot of my teammates who I had worked so hard with were there to share the excitement. The tears started rolling. As the tears were rolling down my face, I was so emotional I just kept repeating "all I wanted was an opportunity; all I wanted was an opportunity." I had never asked anyone to give me anything I didn't earn. I had asked my mom for an opportunity to play pop warner. I wanted an opportunity to play at Adrian College and now biggest of them all— an opportunity to play in the NFL.

I will never forget the second day of the draft as long as I live. My friends were even crying because they knew what I had gone through to even have a shot at the NFL. I was so thankful to have them around for that special day. We went to Applebee's to celebrate and

I think we all needed it. Joel, Barclay, Plaxx— my closest friends—
were all in attendance and it was a great feeling.

CHAPTER 20

─────

ALLEN PARK

IT WAS TIME TO head to Allen Park, Michigan where the Lions facility was located. I walk in and I was amazed by the facility. The first thing I had to do was get a physical, and it covered everything— blood work, EKG, dentistry, you name it. I also had to go in for x-rays because of my prior surgeries. The detail at that level was unbelievable. If you had a cavity they wanted it to be fixed. Some guys were sent home because they didn't pass the physical. I couldn't believe how many tubes of blood that had been taken from me.

What a great environment to be in. It was time for the final step, we had to get our helmets and select our cleats. It was basically Footlocker inside of the Lions facility: any and every cleat you can think of was there. I had to sit on a stool so that they could put my cleats on for me and fit my helmet and facemask that I wanted. Everything was first class. I wore #49 in college and they gave me #48 and it was close enough for me.

After I was done, I was shown my locker, and as I was finishing up Ernie Sims walked in. We stopped to have a conversation and I told him I was excited to be there and asked if he had any advice for me. His response was real simple: work hard. We had a team meeting and this was it—I was in an NFL team meeting with our head coach Rod Marinelli.

Coach Marinelli didn't hold any punches and he made sure everyone in the room understood that this was a business and he wanted good men and not assholes. He told us if we were going to be with the Lions organization you had to do things the right way especially off the field. I heard him loud and clear, during the process I had felt that the guys they were being arrested all of the time were the guys getting all of the damn attention and I didn't understand it all.

The team meeting was over and it was time for our position meeting with Coach Snow, who told us what he expected and that they would be keeping one or two linebackers out of the group. We were given our playbooks and we would be having a practice after dinner and things were about to get real.

We had a chef that was there making food at our request. This was the life in the NFL: we had dinner, meetings, and practice. After practice we would meet again, and then it was time to head to our hotel for a snack. There wasn't time for anything else, I showered and took about 10 minutes to call a few people to let them know how things were going. After that, it was time to study the playbook—I literally went to sleep with my playbook. I woke up at 5:30am to study more and get ready for the day. We would catch the shuttle and it was time to grind. We would not get back to the hotel until about 10pm. I have a tremendous amount respect for Calvin Johnson who was a first round pick and would receive millions of dollars and he was on the shuttle with everyone else, which told me a lot about his character. Joel was a big Lions fan and I told him that Calvin would be a Hall of Fame receiver and he has proven me to be right.

Upon arrival at the facility we would have breakfast, practice and do the same thing for lunch and dinner. On day two, Coach Lyall, Coach Klotz, and Coach Bo all came down to watch us practice and it was great to the see some familiar faces. The last day was upon us and it was time to find out my fate. They decided not to keep me, but instead they went with my roommate and I thought it would be me or Joe who was my roommate or another linebacker from Northwood University.

CHAPTER 21

NEXT

Dᴜʀɪɴɢ ᴛʜᴇ ᴡᴇᴇᴋ I had a conversation with my agent about Plan B to figure out what we would do next after things didn't work out in Detroit. I wanted him to also contact CFL teams to let them know that there was interest. I returned home to Adrian and honestly I was in limbo for a few weeks and nothing was really happening. I decided to get a new agent and I hired the guys out of Atlanta who I had considered before picking the guy out of San Francisco.

They went to work fast, and once again I had another opportunity and this time it was with the Buffalo Bills for a workout, as they were looking for practice squad players. After hearing from Buffalo, I flew out the next day for the workout, and I had been training so I was ready to go. It was a few weeks after I had left Detroit. I would arrive at the hotel to check-in and found out the agenda for the following day.

We had to weigh in and I recall putting on six pairs of socks to make sure my height was 6'1. I know that sounds crazy, but measurements were important in the NFL. There were guys from a lot of different Division 1 programs. This time there would not be a 40 yard dash, short shuttle, or L-Drill—it was all position work. I was the first guy in line for every drill and was feeling great. I told myself before the workout that I was going to be perfect today at that was my attitude. My attitude always dictated the outcome. Drill after drill, I felt like I was turning heads, and the guys behind me knew I could play and I was looking good. You can always tell by the facial expressions, I had been around the game long enough to pick those things up. I was in a zone and everything just felt good and as an athlete you know when you are in the zone.

We wrapped up the workout and I give my new agent a call to tell him that I felt great and I felt like I was one of the best linebackers there, and I really believed that. There are always guys who believe their name and university they played for is enough to get a shot. We got the normal spiel after the workout: "If we are interested we will give you or your agent a call, and thanks for coming out." I would fly out the next morning and hope to hear back from the Buffalo Bills. The weeks would go by and I hadn't heard anything, so I figured they had signed a different linebacker. I would continue to work out, and I even added some of the drills from the Bills workout just in case it was something I had to do again.

CHAPTER 22

MISSED CALL

So much time had passed by and I figured I was not going to hear from Buffalo, although I felt like I was the best linebacker at the workout. A month after the workout with Buffalo I was in the process of changing cell phone providers. I was going from T-Mobile to Nextel as the two-way phones were starting to become really popular. I was beyond frustrated at this point and wasn't sure what the next step would be.

My new phone came in so I activated it and received my new number. I would often leave my old phone in my room. I was back in school at this time to continue working on my degree. The NFL season had started and I was going to class and training. One of the scouts at the All-Star game told us to always be ready, so I was.

It was a normal day. I had gone to class and to the Merillat Center to get my workout in and then I went to dinner. When I returned to my room, something told me to turn on my old phone and I did. It took a few minutes to come on and I had two voicemails. It was from Kevin Meganck from the Buffalo Bills. "Hey Taz it's Kevin Meganck from the Buffalo Bills we wanted to fly you in tomorrow to work you out for a practice squad spot. We liked what you did during your workout. We will be bringing in four linebackers, and you're one of them. Give me a call back ASAP so that we can confirm that you can make it and get you your flight information."

Initially I was excited and I was hoping that the window wasn't closed. You only get so many opportunities in the NFL, and then they move on to the next guy. I called Kevin back over and over again, but unfortunately he had left the office. I didn't sleep at all that night, I played the voicemail to my roommate Barclay and he couldn't believe I had missed the call.   All I could think about was missing that phone call because I knew I had performed well during the first workout. The next morning, I call Kevin at 6 am and still no answer, so I left another voicemail. I call again at 7 am and still nothing, so I left another voicemail. I tried again around 7:50 am and finally I got an answer. "Kevin, it's Taz, I'm sorry I missed your call – I was transitioning to a new phone and I got your voicemail late. I can still make it to Buffalo, you let me know when. "Taz we needed you here by noon, let me see if I can get you a flight out and I'll call you right back." I waited for about 30 minutes and finally I hear back from Kevin. "Taz, it's Kevin. Sorry, we can't get you a flight that will have you here by noon. If anything changes, I will let you know." I was devastated. I couldn't believe I had missed a call from the Bills. I was so pissed at myself for changing phones; I knew that if I went back out to Buffalo I would be signed to the practice squad. That was it—I had blown my opportunity to play in the NFL. I called my agent with the hope that he could get me another workout. They signed a linebacker to the practice squad the same day and he went on to play in the NFL for 8 years.

After that day, I didn't want to be around people. I was actually miserable. In fact, I was so miserable that my voicemail message said "Leave me a message and if I don't call you back that probably means I don't want to talk to you." I became a very dark person because my dream was gone and I knew at that moment that it was over. It wasn't going to be like before when I made a mistake and got back on the right track. I continued to ask myself why I missed that call. I was angry; I had sacrificed everything and I had lost people that I cared about because of my dedication to the game of football.

I had hit rock bottom. I was at the lowest I had ever been in my entire life, and I had grown up in the projects, attended an alternative school, been on probation, and was unable to play as a senior in high school. Even after all of those things, I had never felt so low. *Why me?* The kid who wanted to help his mom just blew it. I let my mom down. She was depending on me to help her and I failed her. I wanted to provide for my mom so badly. She had worked so hard to raise me and provide for me and I let her down. Still to this day, every day that I wake up I think about that missed phone call.

CHAPTER 23

EUROPE

A FEW MONTHS LATER, I went to Europe to play and get more film and I quickly found out that my expectation for the game of football was completely different than Denmark's. I played one game for the Triangle Razorbacks before returning home. There were great people in Denmark, but it was not going to help me get back to the NFL.

I returned home and I was still in a dark place. I had moved in with my uncle because school was out. I would stay in the house for days at a time and not answer any calls. I would distance myself from people because I felt defeated and I wasn't sure what else there was for me to do. My entire life had revolved around the game since I was 9 years old.

My relationships would struggle and I couldn't really be around people. I had been so use to leading people and being the guy who was always lifting everyone up and now I was the guy who was struggling to go outside and have a normal conversation. I broke up with my girlfriend—someone who I really cared about because I was miserable and I felt I had nothing to give anyone else. I couldn't love anyone or hug them or encourage them I was doing my best to make it through the day. I couldn't wrap my head around the fact that my dream would only be a dream. I had gone back to the days of not caring about anything. I was almost at my boiling point. I didn't understand my purpose anymore. I was driven my whole life by the game of football—nothing else motivated me to do better. Football influenced me to finish high school, move away from home, and go to college.

How could this happen? I had no explanations and I didn't really know what to do next. Even when things were at their worst, I had never given up on anything, but I had never been to *this* place. I didn't understand it. I wished that I would've turned that phone on earlier, but I didn't. This was real and there was nothing that I could do to change the current circumstances with the Buffalo Bills.

I didn't want to call my mom and tell her the bad news, but I had no choice because I knew she would ask if I had heard anything. Eventually I told her that I had missed the call and I was hoping for another opportunity.

The opportunity was gone. I couldn't live in misery forever. It was time to pick myself up and move on with life as I had done so many times before. It was just adversity, and I had always found a way before.

CHAPTER 24

NEW OPPORTUNITY

I NEEDED A WAY TO stay involved with the game. I received a call from Coach Klotz and he wanted to know if I was interested in coaching. I definitely was because I needed to be around football, and I was all about helping kids. I went in to meet the head coach at a local high school in Adrian. He offered me the varsity linebacker position and I was beyond excited about the opportunity.

I had never coached a day in my life, but I knew the linebacker position like the back of my hand. I started attending the summer weight lifting sessions when I was able. We had staff meetings and I was impressed with the organization of the program that I was involved with. I found out very quickly that coaching was completely different than playing: having success as a player did not make you a good coach or guarantee any success for that matter. There was a lot of preparation involved with coaching, as one would expect. We had staff meetings, team camps and 7 on 7 to help prepare us for the season. I had been through all of these things as a player but it was still very different.

I was also still pursuing other football opportunities during this time. I was still training as if I was playing, so that if an opportunity came about I was ready to go. My agent was sending out film to every league that was in existence. Coaching gave me a different perspective about the game itself. My appreciation for coaches definitely grew because there are a lot of sacrifices that take place.

I found myself providing the same support that Coach Landrum had provided me during my Westside Raiders days. I had no desire to cheat the game or the kids I was given an opportunity to coach because of the unfortunate circumstances that took place in my career and that gave me the time to do it. It was time to compete in a different way and I was ready for the challenge. We put in a lot of work to make sure our kids were successful.

During my time coaching at the local high school, I was given the opportunity to play in AF2 and the IFL. Both were Arena Leagues. I knew I needed to take advantage of the opportunities that were on the table so that I could hopefully leave the game at some point with a better taste in my mouth when it was over. I also knew I was not signing up for the glamorous lifestyle that I saw in the NFL. There wouldn't be any chefs, five star hotels and the best of the best in terms of equipment and facilities. I was ok with that and I was going to embrace the people and I was going to be all in. I knew no matter what I would have a new set of brothers and that something positive was going to come out of each opportunity.

CHAPTER 25

OVER

I SPENT TWO YEARS PLAYING in AF2 and IFL. Playing Arena football certainly wasn't a part of my plan, but once again my plan didn't mean much. During my time in Ohio I had a chance to build a relationship with Deryck Toles, a former Penn State linebacker. I would always see Deryck meeting with our team's trainer and there was something about him that told me I needed to connect with him. He was a very motivated guy and we had similar backgrounds and little did I know he had an outreach organization that was all about helping the youth called Inspiring Minds and it's still thriving today. Derryck was recognized for his work on Oprah's Ultimate Favorite Things show. We met for lunch one day and developed a relationship, and today he is still someone that I keep in contact with.

During my time in Alaska (my second stop playing arena football) I found out that I was going to be a father and I was immediately done chasing my dream. I would leave for Fairbanks Alaska to play for the Fairbanks Grizzlies and return in June before my daughter was due. I certainly needed something to look forward to and I couldn't wait to become a dad. I had learned what to do and what not do.

June 21, 2010 at 5:21 am my beautiful daughter Londyn was born. My life would change forever and I mean forever. All the energy that I had put into the game of football had now shifted to being a great dad. I was on cloud nine, and even though my playing career was over, I would face new challenges. Shortly after Londyn was born her mom and I decided to go our separate ways. That was tough; I went from seeing her all the time to seeing her sometimes. It was a challenge, but I definitely knew how to deal with adversity.

I decided to pack up and move to Sylvania, Ohio, and it was a much needed move. I spent a lot of time at work and saw Londyn when I was able. Eventually there was a schedule established and I would see Londyn each week and rotate weekends with her mom. I was happy to have things somewhat back to normal. Over the years, things changed and I couldn't be happier. Although her mom and I are no longer together, we really work as a team because we both know it's all about Londyn.

I also met my wife, Rachel, when I was living in Sylvania. Ironically we had both attended Barclay and Steph's wedding back in 2008. Rachel was a friend of the bride and we did not know each other at the time. When Barclay and Steph found out that she was moving to Maumee, Ohio, they thought we would be a good match. After a few phone calls and texts we decided to go out on a date. At the time I was a single dad working 16-hour days and spending any extra time that I had with Londyn. I was certainly not looking for a relationship, but one found me. One day Rachel left her blow dryer and some other things at my house and that was when I knew she was there to stay. After a few weeks I called my friend B.C. and told him that I was going to marry her. That summer we moved in together to a loft apartment.

CHAPTER 26

LIFETIME CONTRACTS

Although I was not able to live out my NFL dream with a contract, the game of football provided me with an overwhelming amount of what I like to call lifetime contracts. I built relationships through the game of football that you cannot put a price on.

I was married in 2014, and my entire wedding party was from college. Most of those same people were there or not far away as I was chasing my dream of playing in the NFL. I also met Carl Singleton during my time in Alaska. Carl flew in from Utah to attend our wedding in Charlevoix, MI. He and his wife, who was his girlfriend at the time, drove five hours from the airport to get to our wedding. It meant the world to me that Carl cared about me that much that nothing was going to stop him from being at my wedding. Even though I never imagined myself doing Arena football, I embraced the opportunity and walked away with more relationships.

I was devastated when things didn't work out for me. Through this disappointment, I discovered a lot about myself I discovered that I was not as strong as I appeared. When the phone stopped ringing,

I wanted to be as far away from people as possible. The relationships from the game that almost destroyed me had given me so much.

Without those lifetime contracts, I'm not sure where I would be today. The game of football broke me down and built me back up with the things that it has provided for me. So many young men walk away from the game feeling empty and unappreciative of the things that the game gives them, and I was no exception.

I wanted something, and individually I received more than what I was asking for. That was the reward. Those people had no idea I needed them during some of the darkest moments of my life, because I didn't express that to them.

I was asked by a family member if I wanted to transfer after my sophomore season at Adrian College and I quickly declined. I wasn't willing to walk out on the people that had cared about me before I was an All-American and the school's All-Time leading tackler. I had brothers and father figures that were counting on me and there was no way in hell I was going to let them down. Life is all about relationships—you can have all of the money in the world but be extremely poor in your relationships. The relationships that I developed were just as important as an NFL contract.

I gave the game everything I had. Sometimes, things don't go your way, but you have to keep scratching and clawing or you will be left with nothing. I'm a better man today because of the game of football. The game had also consumed me so much that my relationships struggled. For a brief moment, I felt unworthy because I didn't accomplish my childhood dream. That was the moment that I looked in the mirror and said to myself I must do what I've always done: fight.

I have no regrets and I still have the same love for the game as I did when I was a little boy. I learned how to be accountable, self-disciplined, and I also learned to deal with adversity. I have had several obstacles since that missed call, and I would like to think that the missed call allowed me to overcome adversity.

CHAPTER 27

FAMILY

I NEVER PLAYED ONE DOWN in the NFL, but the chase taught me so much. Today I am a husband and the father of two beautiful little girls. Those times that I watched Coach Klotz and Coach Lyall interact stuck with me. That same work ethic that was applied to the game is now applied to my family. I still love the game of football and I also have a ton of respect for it.

I thought it was breaking me down disappointment after disappointment, but what the game was really doing is preparing me for the life that I was about to live. I would not be the person I am today if it wasn't for the process that I had to go through with football. I had been to the lowest I had ever been in my life and I survived. I found a way, and that's life. I didn't expect my father figures Klotz and Lyall to be perfect, and neither am I. I can tell you that my life has been built from relationships. I was relentless in my pursuit to be the school's all-time leading tackler and a great captain and teammate, and I did that.

Now, it's about being the best husband that I can be to my beautiful wife Rachel and the best dad that I can be to my girls Londyn and Evie. I didn't know why I missed the call at the time, but I understand now that it's normal for society to think the NFL is the cream of the crop. I had a greater purpose than the one that I set out for myself, and I believe I'm a better person because of it. I cherish every moment that I'm around my family and those that are close to me.

I love going to Londyn's gymnastics class and all I want is for my kids to grow and have a work ethic, value relationships, and to always scratch and claw. I hope that we are able to teach them that life is not easy and there will be adversity along the way, but never give up. My 3-year-old is too young to understand, but I always tell my oldest daughter Londyn that if she wants to be her best, she will have to work, and there is no other way around it. Being an involved father is important to me. I want my girls to be able to stand on their own two feet and understand that they will always have to earn things in life, and that requires me to be honest with them and love them unconditionally. Everything they do is important to me and they are my number one priority. I understand that I play a major role in helping them create their identity. The thing that I'm most proud of today is that my kids will never go through what I went through and that they know dad is there for them. That's more important than any tackle that I've ever made.

It's my responsibility to stay involved in the game as long as I can and help mold young men of character as all of my coaches have done for me. You are who you are. Mckenzie Court created my identity early: I was tough, respectful and hardworking. I would have loved to play in the NFL, but the relationships that I have are invaluable and the game provided that for me and I'm forever grateful. I wanted to be a good teammate above all else. I'm very proud of the lifetime contracts that I have and they can never be taken from me.

Life will always provide us with opportunities to give up, tap out, or quit—choices we as individuals have to make.

Coach Lyall promised me two things before I decided to come to Adrian College: we would compete for championships, and I would earn a degree. He should've also promised that he would be in my life forever because we still have a great relationship today. He's definitely like a dad to me and I always talk to him before I make any big decisions. Although we never won the MIAA title during my time, we had opportunities to do so. He is someone that has had a huge impact on me as a person.

Coach played football at the University of Michigan. He always told us he wasn't a great player, but he worked extremely hard and built great relationships during his time at Michigan. He also built his program at Adrian College on relationships. I've never seen anyone at a Division 3 school recruit the way Coach Lyall did. He brought in 75 to 100 players each year and we played at a high school stadium. He did it because he was as genuine as they come. Coach also had high expectations for us as people and players.

I recall being late to a meeting during my sophomore year at Adrian. My teammates and I had a system to make sure everyone made it out of the dorm together on time. Unfortunately one day that system failed. My teammates came into my room at 5:45 am to make sure I was up. Upon opening the door, they didn't see me in my room, but I was certainly there. The crew headed to morning conditioning and I was still in my dorm on the top bunk sleeping. I finally woke up and sprinted to the Merillat Center where we held morning conditioning. There was a team meeting afterward and I knew better than attempting to go into the meeting late. Coach Lyall is a great guy, but he had high expectations for his players. It didn't matter who you were, and that's what I loved about him. As I sat in the lobby waiting for the meeting to be over I knew things were going south real fast. Coach Lyall exited the meeting and wanted to see the guys that were late in his office one at a time. He told me that I was last and that wasn't good. I sat in the lobby waiting my turn and I knew I better not attempt to make an excuse about being late. The first guy went, the second guy went, and then it was my turn. Coach Lyall said "what the hell are you doing being late?" He also used some other choice words and he told me that he was disappointed in me and it better not happen again. I also had to come in to see Coach Bo our DL coach for some additional morning workouts that included burpees on a pole vault pit, and that experience was awful. I was never late again and even today I like to be 10 minutes early wherever I go.

That's who coach is, he loved us as players but he put a huge emphasis on teaching us to be men. I never held a grudge against coach after that dreaded meeting, but I did learn a valuable lesson and how important it was to be on time. Coach is very important to me and he's certainly someone I admire. He stood up in my wedding and he also attends our kids' birthday parties and it means a lot to me. Coach took care of me and changed my life. Now it's my turn, so I often call him or send a text to see how he and Mrs. Lyall are doing.

CHAPTER 28

GROWTH

In 2010, I became the Athletic Director/Behavior Specialist at a Morenci High School. It was my first big job and I was very excited and humbled. I was chosen out of over 40 applicants. I had no experience in the field, and I hadn't finished my degree. Still, I walked into the interview confident in my abilities to lead. I also learned during this process that people must create opportunities for themselves. It all goes back to relationships—I had no experience, but I did have a list of people that could speak to my character and who I was as a person. I saw this as an opportunity for me to grow personally and professionally. I jumped right in— one of the first things I did was write a letter to the staff about who I was and how excited I was to have an opportunity to work in the district. To be completely honest, I know there were some people who did not want me working in the district. I didn't let those things bother me, I chose to embrace them because I was there to serve the people, and again my perception of others came from how they treated me and the people around me.

I believe that anytime you are in a leadership role, you can't be concerned with who likes you or doesn't like you. I was focused on being the best AD I could be for the student-athletes I was serving. I had to make some big decisions early on, and some didn't like it. I always understood that people have a right to their opinion, and I was okay with that.

The first year went well, and I believe we grew as an athletic department. At the end of the football season, our head coach at the time decided to retire. To be completely honest with you, I had never planned to be in education. We may have a plan for what we want to do, but our purpose is sometimes more important than our plan.

I decided to apply to be the Head Football Coach. I submitted my resume and other materials that pertain to coaching. I went through the interview process and I became head coach at the age of 28. I was ecstatic to be back coaching after taking a year off when I became the Athletic Director.

It was time to go to work. In the coming weeks I would build a staff and start our strength and conditioning program. With the support of our administration, I was also able to create a team room so that we had a permanent place to meet and watch film. We were behind in a lot of areas; for example, we still had VHS when most people had transitioned to DVD.

My first year as a head coach was a great experience, and I definitely grew. We finished 5-4 and had a chance to get to the playoffs. Unfortunately, we lost in the first round of the playoffs. The plan was to give the players time off before we started preparing for the next season. As I mentioned earlier, our purpose is sometimes more important than our plan.

CHAPTER 29

MY TURN

DURING THE SEASON WE played Madison (my alma-mater), and after the game one of the Madison parents came up to me and said I needed to come back and coach at Madison. I guess she knew something that I didn't at the time. I had no intentions of going to Madison and quite honestly it wasn't something that I had ever thought about. I was offered a few assistant coaching opportunities with the football team in previous years, but it wasn't the right time for me.

After the season, the head coaching position at Madison became open. I didn't waste any time going after it. I reached out to the Superintendent and expressed my interest. It was perfect timing as the high school principal was looking to add a Student Success Coach. It would obviously have to be something that I was interested in and confident doing. It also had to be the right fit for me and the school. Things moved fast; I met with the administration and we talked about the position in the building. I was recommended to be hired as the Student Success Coach and Head Football Coach.

I was very excited to return to Madison—it was a great place with great people. I felt like it was my turn to give back to a school and community that had supported me during my time in high school and in college. I recall the unbelievable support that I received at Madison, a place that certainly helped mold me. There were always people showing up to my college games. It seemed like the Roesch brothers were always on the road and their support meant the world to me.

I'm currently still serving at Madison. My position is very interesting. I see so many young men that remind me of me. The plan for me to mentor kids was part of my purpose in life and I have embraced that role. We are living in a society today where kids simply want someone to care about them. I tell the kids that I say what they need to hear and not what they want to hear. There is nothing a kid can tell me that I haven't experienced or seen before, so we are able to eliminate the "can't" in all of our conversations. I'm always very happy to tell them I don't understand the "I can't" mentality. I can speak from experience and I believe that allows me to build relationships with the students. That is the foundation for having any type of success in the classroom.

CHAPTER 30

11 YEARS

I OBVIOUSLY LEFT SCHOOL EARLY to chase my dreams, and that meant I was risking my degree. It was worth the risk, and I definitely don't regret making that decision. While going through the process to make it to the NFL, I knew if I made it or didn't make it I would need a college degree to be successful in life. As many say, NFL stands for "Not For Long". I've never known "easy" and completing my degree wasn't any different, it took me 11 years to get a four-year degree, and I'm not embarrassed to say that.

So many things were happening in my life and I simply put my degree on the back burner. I had a new job that was very demanding, and I was a new dad who had been playing football and basically living out of a suitcase for two years. I often thought that I had come too far not to complete my college degree. It was always on my mind to get it done, but unfortunately I may have been on cruise control because I had a decent job and my degree wasn't complete, I was very honest during the interview process about where I was in terms of completing my degree.

I came to a point where I told myself "it's time to get it done." It took a lot of positive self-talk. I wanted my daughters to see that I had finished what I started and that was important to me. My degree didn't have a date on it but they would know that I got it done. I needed to complete seven credit hours and I would finally be done. I searched for a few weeks to find a school where credits would transfer to Adrian College. After my intense search, I was able to find a school and I was ready to get work.

I took my first college course in August of 2003 and I received my degree from Adrian College in 2014. I don't recommend this approach, but it was how things happened for me. I've always had to find a way to get things done. I've never loved school, and I was very happy to receive my degree because I knew what it took to get it. Most of the time our path in life is not a straight road: there are a lot of turns, stop signs, and temporary road blocks but it always goes back to choosing to do or not to do something. I was able to accomplish something that I didn't grow up seeing a lot of people accomplish. I've learned in life that no one owes you anything and anything worth having has a price tag on it and you must be willing to pay that price to get what you want.

There will be another person that goes through the same struggles that I went through. I encourage you to find a way and be the best version of you that you can be. Life is not about settling and accepting what people give you. It's important that you go out and chase your dreams and create your own identity. You owe it to yourself, and the world owes you nothing. Whatever you choose to do, use the opportunity and don't let the opportunity use you. I encourage you to build as many meaningful relationships as possible and surround yourself with people who want to see you happy. Life is hard and it should be. Refuse to be entitled and understand that you will always deal with adversity regardless of your education and socioeconomic status. I hope that you find happiness and joy in life that will be long-lasting and enjoyable for you and the people you are around. The game that almost broke me also provided me with the tools that I needed to overcome adversity and be the best version of myself. I can say with confidence that I would be dead or in jail if it weren't for football. Life is about relationships. Take time to invest in those relationships, those people that truly care about you will always push you to be your best.

The perception may be that the guy from Tuscaloosa has made it, let me be the first to tell you that I haven't. I still operate as if I'm still in the projects trying to find a way out, and I want more out of life. There is no time to for complacency. There will be people along the way who may be smarter than me and who grew up in a better environment than me, but I will always outwork them. I'm not satisfied to be where I am in life today. I still have more work to do, and that's my focus.

Whatever you choose to do, dedicate every fiber in your body to becoming the best version of yourself. Thank you for taking the time to read my story.

Don't waste anytime hoping invest all of your time into working. Hope is for average people... work is for those striving for greatness.

BEFORE YOU GO....

I would love to hear from you! Please share your favorite chapters, quotes, and excerpts on Twitter. Tag me and use #thegame.

Twitter: @Coach_Wallace83

For inquires about the book, to schedule speaking engagements, or for team or group orders contact:

Tavarski Wallace

thegtabm@gmail.com